Dancing

in a

Minefield

Dancing In a Minefield

Hope Hill

Dancing in a Minefield
Copyright © 2020 by Hope Hill. All Rights Reserved.
No part of this publication may be reproduced, stored, distributed, or transmitted by any means including photocopying, recording, or other electronic or mechanical methods without prior written consent and permission of the author except as provided by USA copyright law.

ISBN: 979-8678450968

Printed in the United States of America
Cover Copyright by Hope Hill
Cover design by selfpubbookcovers.com

Dedicated to Chico Library's Open Mic Group, NaNoWriMo and anyone who's ever used poetry as therapy.

The drumming in my head
Is thrumming in my feet
I cannot explain the way
I'm synced into the beat
It's over now until
The second hand is still
Would that I was not alone
In feeling all emotion
There is much to do
And I will not shirk away
From feeling these emotions
Sweeping over me
It takes a lot to get lost
Inside another's music
True to form I learned my lyrics
By listening to
The rhythm of the trees

My world is crazy
My thoughts are too
It's time to chance
The final dance
Time to take the inspiration
Pluck it from the sky

No one has to know
If you are free from insanity
I'm racing the calendar
Cause if I can escape it
The reward is greater
Than you'll ever know
Do you see the darkness
Lurking in my words?
And with the shields fallen
The scent of my insanity
Lingers in the air
It almost seems to taunt me

With the knowledge it looms closer
With every waking day
I'm hiding 'neath the anger
Of one who has been wronged
I'm choking back the screams
Of my inner child and memories
I feel that I'm not present
In my real life
Why am I spectating 'stead of living?
What would it take
To scrub off all the shame?
Some days it seems
Even peeling off my skin
Might not be enough
I'm afraid to write
For fear of what I'll say
Or worse yet
Will admit
There's no way that I can hide
When you've found out the truth
No way to push it back

I cannot explain
This temperamental force
I'm trying to be fair
To all that I can see
It's hard to reconcile
The calming
With the sea
It all can go away
If you know how to ask
The worlds are at
Your fingertips
Not a single wasted day
Has ever crossed the line
Between your world and mine
Sad as it might seem
Most cannot remain
In their changeling state
It's much too hard
For most adults
To enter a childlike state
They don't know how
To stay this FEY

I wish you knew
The worlds I've been
And how I've stayed this way
My imagination never went away
My simple zest for life
And curiosity were enough
To make me seek out
Second generation selkies
And what became of unicorns
When we first disbelieved
Were the ogres nice at first
Before we told them not to be?
What would our world be like
If the creatures took back their world?
Are there mermaids who hate water?
And what about mermen?
Can you become a creature
Or is it up to fate
To determine what our species is?
Who knows what I'll find out
In my quest for mythical legacies?

Does any author have it right?
Is it really make believe?
Is that just how it seems?
My world is full of questions
And no-one has the answers

I am my own enigma
That no-one else
Can truly understand
Is this my fate in life
To always ask what others
Only dare to dream of?
But I've journeyed to other worlds
Even if only in my head
And with my gift for words
I'm sure that I can
Bring along a friend
As long as they agree
To suspend their disbelief
Will you agree to be that friend
And venture forth with me?
I'd like the company

To tell the truth
My travels have been getting lonely
I'm sure that I can venture farther
If someone else comes with me
I'll even let you pick the galaxy
I'm tired of this world
With its simplicity
I'm looking for a place
With magic in its veins
I need to see the things
I've been dreaming of since birth
Maybe you can find my kind
And rescue me from earth
There's not a day
That I don't wish for more
Than this solitary existence
I know I've got my love
And a family's assistance
But I don't feel connected
To the world I was born in

My enemy is stronger
Than anything you've seen
I'm fighting despair and apathy
no-one knows the danger
Of these simple things
Till they've seen
Hope and empathy in action
Will you now explain the cost
Of losing all interest
In creativity and positivity?
I'm looking at bleak flowers
Wishing I could bring the rain
It always seems to cheer me
And wash away the pain
I don't need to tell you
That I've seen more
Than you can imagine
Of tears falling like rain
What I would give
To make sure that the living
Would always be giving
More than they take

And showing the world
The meaning of faith
I swear I am persistent
In my search for life
I know that somewhere out there
Is a reason for everyone
To want to live
It seems so simple
On days when life is good
To think of why you should
Stick with it till the end
But on days when life is dark
And everything is hard
It can seem overwhelming
And it's easier to give in
Than to wait for things to change
My path is certain
I must make the world
A different place
Than it was 'ere I was born
I aim to understand
The trials we all face

I cannot claim to help
Till I know the troubles
Of the human race
It is a struggle to keep up the pace
I wish to stop this flood of words
But without the poetry
I might give up the race
Life's a battle
I'm not winning
But if I don't give up
Half the battle has been won

Tell me truly
Do you know me?
Can you explain
Why I must pour out these words
Or risk losing my sense of self?
I know who and what I am
Can you say the same
In this day and age?
Does anyone else see
Why we struggle to survive?

To pick up the flag
And help out those who've fallen

My life's been rearranged
By the beating of the drums
And I wouldn't mind
If the person drumming was me
I can handle change
But I need a reason to do so
Without a chance to type
My mind would be long gone
I wish you'd seen the promise
Floating in the sky
Would you have waited
For it to get better
Rather than slip away
Like a shadow in the night?
I wish you'd never gone away
Wish I never had to say
That you'd never wake again
I can't afford
To lose myself in grief

And even if I could
It wouldn't do me good
My pain walks out the door
And I'm afraid to follow

Whatever's in my head
Will wind up on the page
For emotions without end
Can send you in a rage
My writing cannot end
For I will surely wither
Without a chance to dither

Trinkets and broken dreams
Placed in the same box
That no-one's cleaned in years
Homework and past regrets
Make up my childhood memories
It's hard to remember
The way I used to be
But even then I only dreamed
Of one day being told

"I'll protect you for always
no-one will hurt you again"
Then given a hug,
A kiss on the head,
And tucked into bed
I wasn't the brightest of kids
But even I knew
That's what parents
Are supposed to do
I shouldn't have been jaded
At the age of ten
And at thirteen
My biggest fear
Should've been not having
The right jeans to wear
Instead I faced horrors
No child should have to
From people I was told
I could trust not to hurt me
Needless to say
I lost that naivete

Much to my chagrin
I had to start again
Different family,
Different town
Not that it mattered much
The past; it chose to haunt me
The anger just kept growing
My faith could not keep up
It was shrunken and tired
From trying to make sense of
A pain children were
Never meant to know
Knowing what would happen
Only made it harder
To tell the truth
And set myself free
Of the chains holding me back
From becoming the woman
I was always meant to be
When nothing holds me back
What exactly will I do?

Who's to say
I can't reach my dreams
Or go see another lost planet
Why should I dream small?
Someday I'll be
Everything I dreamed of
I only need to try
I'm just another child
Who grew up too fast
I want you to imagine
A world without fear
What would it be like?
Would everyone be reckless
Or just without malice and strife?
Would anyone be hurtful?
Would they still know anger and pain?
Would they recognize a teardrop?
What creatures would live there?
What about their plant life?
Would they still need Willow trees?
Is it hard to comprehend
What our lives would be like

If they were never touched by fear?
Which other emotions if any
Might we also lose if we felt no fear?
It would take an angel's breath away
To see the world without pain
For even a single day

I know what is happening
Much as I might wish to deny it
I've seen this all before
My mind has conquered this before
Not that you would know it
If you saw me quaking in fear
Rocking takes the pain away
I need to hear them say
Everything will be alright someday
I don't care if they lie
I only need to not pass out or cry
My memories are torturing
The inside of my mind
It seems like they are stabbing
The inner child that I hide

I hide behind these lofty words
And hope they'll be enough
To lure you off in another direction
So I'll survive to enter
The bunker full of books
I'm shielded at the Library
Though it may be full of kooks
Do not attempt to understand
The things I'm typing now
For even I know not
The reasons for this griping

I'm frightened once again
Of the metaphorical pen
I have to rhyme once again
Or face the dreaded red pen
How fearful of its crimson stain
Just remembering can cause me pain
I need to just step back
From everything I'm hiding from
It's times like this that I become
The person I hate most

I want you all to know
There was nothing you could do
We all feel pain at times
The only difference between me and you
Is that when I'm terrified to sleep at night
It's because of what I'll remember
Rather than just a bad dream
Nothing scares me more
Than what I've already faced
No new illusions I just won't face
Maybe if I listen to the music
Of a dying race
I'll forget about my troubles
This seems much too dark and serious
I must change the tone and pace

So hard to write for hours
When you cannot tell a soul
The truth about your feelings
And why you've become
An emotional black hole
Most of my misadventures

Started with another's misconceptions
Want to see me flounder
You only have to watch me swim
I don't need your irreverence today
I'll leave the chaos alone today
Someone else can be your confessor
I've nothing more to say

I can't heal you till I'm whole
I leaped off the edge of the cliff last night
Fortunately someone left a trampoline
On a low hanging ledge
So I bounced right back up
Watch me tap dance
At the edge of reason
Tiptoe over the line
Of insane recollection
Some things are easier to
Acknowledge than others
I want to be happy
I know you do too
Is it so wrong

To wish and dream
Instead of hate and scheme?
Must I become mainstream
In order to be liked and appreciated?

Nothing I tell you in confidence
Is ever as sacred
As what I don't say
My journal's not private
But if you can read this
Promise me one thing
Save your judgments till the end
Don't accuse me of anything
Until you've read every last letter

I'm inspired by the tipping and tapping
Of the fifty odd students
Typing in a campus library,
Some work on homework,
Some are playing games,
Some are reading or watching,
Me I'm writing free verse poetry

I wish to hear the siren's call
Causing me write in thrall
I wonder which words
I'd be inspired to scribe
If I had to write or lose my life?

A poem a day
Can make me go crazy
A chance to miscommunicate
Has strangely come my way
Should I attempt to take advantage?
Will anything stay the same?
Will I regret the things I've done
Or will I merely learn to live
With what I have become ?
I cannot mask my madness
But I can make you think
That it's a worthwhile thing
Do not expect a miracle from me
I cannot correctly counsel everyone
Most days I do not even try
After all I don't know how to fly

And much as I might try
It is not worth the consequence
Of my insides coming out

It's time to admit
Where I've been,
What I've done
I can't say that I'll outrun
The coldness in my heart
But what I can't admit
Some days I wish to run
From the feelings you impart
There's no reason to feel fear
And I know I hold you dear
I only know you can't help
The way you feel inside
I may not be typically romantic
But one thing I know is true
It could take a lifetime
For me to get over loving you
I'll tell you a secret
no-one else knows

When it comes to you
I have no defenses
I've told you all I know
And in talking told you more
You know me better than anyone
Since you know me so well
I have to let it all spill out
There are parts of me
no-one's seen before
And I think you'll bring them out
Is anything so wonderful or terrible
As the truth of who and what you are?

My intuition may make or break me
Although I'd never let that show
I'm dancing on the tightrope
Questioning when I shall fall
Over and under the waterfall
Of fluid insanity
Do you like my stream
Of odd, chaotic consciousness?
Have you learned and grown with me?

In ways you never knew you could
Should I embrace the darker side
Of life and what it made of me?
Disgust me with your apathy
And I'll return with empathy
That most elusive of emotions
One which most never fully explore

My world is such
That anyone can join
If they can only find the door
Take me at my word
For I am nothing without it
No longer exiled
From proper company
Yet still I dare not linger
Else I'll be forced to mingle
What of this chaos make thee?
In my vilified company
Will I always be expected
To make light of
My lack of ambition

Or is that merely
The status quo for now?
I seem so lyrical
In my
Ebbing depression,
Clinical analysis and dissection
Of my inner and outer selves
Would that I was not so into
Brutally honest self-expression
Sincere though I might be
I do not expect thee
To listen only when I speak
Or not heed others
When absent I must be
Do not make me
The villain in my own tale
Though I know truly
I may never be a hero
Even if I write the book
My nature is not villainous
Merely chaotic in a way
Most have never seen before

I shall redefine myself
As barely confined chaos
Much of my circumspection
Stems from once upon a times
The world is neither
Purely good nor purely evil
It is a fascinating contrast
Of these opposing forces
And any others that wish to tag along
Some of these others are known as
Chaos, Nature, Chemistry, Order,
True Neutral, Truth
And creatures whose names
We were never meant to know

Even through the tears I hide
I am letting something through
no-one has to feel it too
I only sing this song to you
Tell me if you've heard
The songs I've sung
To the dead and dying?

When no-one was around to care
If I was breaking all conventions
Mistakes I felt were all too real
Time again I've helped you heal
Even with no end in sight
I couldn't make you see the light
no-one forces you to see
What you do not wish to see
We only hope that you will learn
Before you're really getting burned
Much as I might wish
I cannot force the truth on you

My life began in darkness
I lived there for years
I can't remember
All of my childhood
Much of it is shrouded in darkness
Memories so painful
I can't recall them
Leaving darkness in their place
A darkness I can't face

I fear this darkness
But more than that
I fear one day
These memories
Will be thrust into the light
Where I cannot hide from them anymore
Some things
Once seen can't be unseen
If I remember
I may not be able
To forget again

I'm dancing in a minefield
Twirling amidst the explosions
Wondering when I'll shatter
And fall apart once more

Poetry is carved into my soul
It seeps into my bones
My heartbeat speaks in verse
My breath a free verse staccato
I am made of metaphor

I could no more cease writing
Than I could unmake myself
This is the remix edition
The first version rewritten

My first love is gone
She was reborn as me
I didn't love her
When she was there
It was only in her absence
That I learned her worth
Only after she died
And I was reborn
From the ashes
That I learned to love her
And I've grieved for her ever since
I was her
But I can't be her
And that's the saddest truth I know

I am broken

In ways that can never be fixed

I cannot be cured

Though there are some

Who'd try

PTSD is the nightmare

From which I cannot wake

The thing that's stolen

Things that were not its to take

You can call me a victim

It has the benefit of being true

Or call me a coward

For being unable to defend myself

Carve it on my tombstone

If you must

But never claim

That I chose not to fight

I've suffered long and hard

And I will suffer more

It does not beckon me to peace

It beckons me to war

But I will go

And I will fight
And then I'll fight some more
I cannot say how I will die
But I will always fight
I will not go quietly into the night
I cannot do so anymore
I spent too long in silence
So when I started speaking
I'd forgotten how to whisper
I can only shout
I was there
I exist

They cannot hurt me anymore
I never asked for this
But no-one ever does
I was young and helpless
And they stole my possibilities
Locked me into a fate
I never wanted
Murdered the girl I wished to be
Took away her future

And blamed me for her death
I watched myself die
And if there'd been any justice
They'd have been found
Looming over our corpse
With our blood on their hands
If they'd found us in time
Perhaps she would have lived
And I wouldn't exist
Would not have
Stepped out of her ashes
Into her shoes
And taken her place
Only to wait
Wondering if one day
I too would die
Only to watch in horror
As the next one in line
Steps out of my ashes
Steps into my shoes
And takes my place
Wondering if one day

She too will share my fate
To die and watch another
Take her place
This to me
Is PTSD
To die and be reborn
Remembering your murder
Unable to forget or move on
Constantly fearing
Whatever killed you,
Remade you in your own image
Forced you to wear the visage
Of a murder victim
Who didn't manage to stay dead
I am still afraid
Of things I can't always explain

Because I died
As surely as if they'd
Taken a gun to my head
And pulled the trigger

They murdered my future
Ripped away my chance at normality
Stole motherhood from me
Made woman
Into a dirty word
Something to be ashamed of
Something to fear
Made it hard to love myself
Made my reflection
Frighten me
They taught me
To feel afraid
That anyone can hurt me
Taught me
That darkness conceals monsters
That walk on two legs
And look like everyone else
That the biggest lie
Is that safety is guaranteed
They made me afraid to leave home
And afraid to stay inside

I have been so scared
Of the people inside four walls
I'd rather take my chances
With a murderer on the loose
Than stay inside
Where I know
Someone wants to hurt me
At least in the dark, alone
With a murderer on the loose
There's a chance I won't be harmed
Anytime I become less afraid
Of a killer on the loose
Than someone inside four walls
I will leave my supposed sanctuary
And take my chances in the dark

What do you do
When you're living a nightmare?
How do you keep those dreams
From coming true?
What do you do

When your monsters are real?
How do you wake
When the nightmare is real?
How do you stop feeling afraid
When the things you fear
Are devastating and real?
How do you live without fear
When the monsters
Walk amongst you
And look like everyone else?
When the worst of your demons
Calls you by name
When the thing you fear most
Wears a face that looks
Far too much like yours?

How do you sleep
When the thing you fear most
Is yourself
In a future
Where you've lost the battle

And the war
Where you abandon
The last shreds of your sanity
And are left with
An eternity alone
With the monsters
Lurking in your mind
And no end to the fight
When all that is left
Is the broken and bruised
Version of you
That's run out of fight
Too damaged to heal
And that future
You fear
Could so easily
Come true?
What do you do
When the only one
Who can end you
Is you?

Closed off, afraid
To say the words
For fear that
I will not be heard
It doesn't matter anyway
They wouldn't understand
What I have to say
No-one listens anymore
I never win my silent war
There's so much left unspoken
Will it leave me broken?
I am all the puzzle pieces
I have ever unlocked
Do I even have the key
To unlock my mystery?

The world
Is a deep, dark, scary place
And I,
I fit right in
So tell me your secrets
The ugly ones

You won't admit

The ones that make you cry

For you

Are no better

Than I

In fact

I find you worse

I at least

Admit my crimes

You shirk from yours

As if your denial

Changes anything

You carry your guilt,

Your shame around

As if that makes you better

You talk

Hypocrisy and self-delusion

Coating every one

Of your words

You are a loathsome thing

And I pity you

Have you ever
Fallen asleep
After the sun came up
So when the nightmares come
As they always do
You'll wake less afraid?
So the coat
Hanging in your closet
Is just a coat
Rather than a menacing stranger
Or even worse
Someone you remember
Trying to kill you
Have you ever died
And stood up afterwards?

Take me away
To a rainy day
Where anything is possible
Where everything's made new
I cry with the sky
As I bathe in the tears

Falling from the sky
Tell me the truth
Do you cry too
When tears fall from the sky?
Do you long for rain
So it covers your pain?
Are you tired too
Of laughing when you want to cry,
Of sealing everything inside,
Everything you're supposed to hide?
I wonder what you'd do
If you could see me now?
The girl I was before
Isn't with us anymore

Silence falls across the walls
No-one hears it's secret calls
Take a walk on the wild side
As you swing from vine to vine
In the jungle of my mind
My strength is as sure as the sun
But I have seen an eclipse

Stomp
Stomp, bang
Stomp, bang, crash
Stomp, bang, crash
Is a melody

Tired of the lies you propagate
Tired of dealing with all of your hate
I bury my pain
And mask it with rage
You tell me I can't escape
But I know those words are fake
Family is a chain I am willing to break

I carry the wounds of my past
They follow me back
As I chart my path
Everything I write
Is tinged in sadness
Even my laughter sounds bitter

I can't write a happy ending
I'm not sure I believe in them
I'm trying to write myself
A happy ending
But everything I write
Is tinged in sadness
Even in fiction
I add in darkness
Unable to believe
In light without shadows

My mind it wanders endlessly
Like a leaf caught in a breeze
My thoughts are stormy like the sea
Ever searching for the key to me
As I write I find the truth
For I have answers I must find
And they are hidden in my mind
Words are dancing through my mind
What secrets hide behind my eyes?
Does my experience make me wise?
I wonder if you'll ever know

How hard it's been for me to grow
I know myself far too well
I'm running from my past pell-mell
You say they're only scary dreams
But they're as real as my screams

I am more than what I was
I cry when the willow tree does
I find hope within the rain
Its cries absolve us all of pain
And children wailed
As proof they failed
Time and time again they lied
Saying you'd be over it if you'd tried
There's no excuse
For such abuse
With every hurt and sting
My tormentors would sing
I felt like an out of water fish
And escaping them was my only wish
These words they do not matter
For I am as mad as a hatter

Forgive, forget a sad refrain
Haunted memories still remain

Tear soaked willow trees
Can my pain ease
A thousand secrets in your eyes
Your pain is always in disguise
So many questions I must ask
As I in your attention bask
Day by day I'm going crazy
I find math inside a daisy
The words they flow onto the page
Oft in sorrow or in rage
The words are dancing to my tune
Inspiration comes morning, night, & noon
The muse of fright
Has been stalking me at night
She never leaves
Just to me cleaves
Nightmares without end
I don't break I merely bend
My future's a bottomless pit of uncertainty

Once again a summer friend
When winter comes with this all end?
I cannot wait for time to tell
If things will go fair or fell
With this much at stake
Something is bound to break
I have to know
Where I should go

I am frightened
I fear my health is fading
I dream of terrors
That I've lived through
And terrors yet to come
Of hospitals and dying
Of something unknown
An unseeable force
That cannot be fought
Today I look into the abyss
Hoping I have a future
Somewhere in those shadows

Deep down I know
Fear has never truly left me
It clings to me
A daily reminder
Of PTSD
My invisible illness
And the pain I feel daily
As ever present as my shadow
And the haunting memories
I fear will never leave me
My eyes betray me
Telling others the secrets
I can never forget
That I have long known pain
In many forms
That I am still afraid
To open up the doors
Inside my mind

Drift into sleep
Like rain on the sidewalk
Tomorrow will keep

You're not on the clock

It's time to dream

Cast your worries aside

Things aren't what they seem

When dreams arrive

Follow your heart

See where it leads

Is there a part

Where I fit your needs?

Each tear I shed

Holds part of me

And when I cry

It finds release

There are hidden parts of me

And with each tear

I set them free

Tears are often near

My tears make waterfalls

I am broken
The breaks will never heal
I pull myself together
Returning to an even keel
Words are all the therapy
I'll ever need

The world is passing me by
But I am frozen in time
Part of me will always be
Stuck in the past that made me
Into this version of me
I am the current incarnation of myself
I have always had this name
But I haven't always been the same
I remember the time before I died
And all the tears I cried
This has taken a dark turn
It's too dark for me
I'd rather not use this ink
To make myself bleed
I prefer flights of fancy

And purple prose
These words are my confession
That I have a heart
And it bleeds sometimes

How do I forgive myself
For dying and getting up again?
Have you ever prayed for rain?
So you could
Release your pain
As your tears mixed with the rain?
My tears are falling rain

I have always been a writer
I turned equations
Into poetry
And poetry
Into equations

For what is Haiku
But another equation
Written in verse

Rhythms and rhymes
Are examples of patterns
Ones I can decipher
With the slightest of ease
Let me take you
Into poetic flow
As I try to show you
They way my mind goes
With poetry and prose
Is it as hard
For you to understand me
As it is
For me to understand you?
Social interaction
Feels like a language
I barely understand
That everyone else can speak
Even explaining

That I don't understand
Requires words you don't know
And may not understand
If I tell you who I am
Will you listen?

A knock at the door
A woman opens the door
As wide as her heart
And gestures in her friend
And the strange child
Holding a black trash bag
The woman asks her friend
If there's anything else
Her friend hands her a folder
She says she's running late
She leaves
Closing the door
On another chapter
Of the child's life
The child stands there
Clutching the trash bag

Blinking back tears
As they stare at the door
"Are you hungry?"
The woman asked
The child nodded
"Spaggetti's in the fridge.
Help yourself. It's your home too."
The woman promised
The child's eyes filled with doubt
But they did not argue
They made themselves a plate
Accepting the food
As the olive branch it was

I am blue and green
In equal measure
Artist and analyst
To the same degree
Can you see
The way I see?
Can you be
A dichotomy?

Or will you stay

A one-way street?

Can you feel the acid

Of all your unshed tears?

Does it burn

When you don't cry?

Feel the heat behind your eyes

But you can never cry

Tired of watching

Everything that I say

Because the truth

Will only cause you pain

Honestly I'm not okay

I'm afraid to fall asleep

For fear of what I'll dream

Or worse remember

I'm always on the verge

Of freaking out

Always on the verge

Of breaking down

I don't wanna go outside

There's so many triggers there
But I can't stay inside forever
Have to face my fears sometime

If you see me
Having a panic attack
Do not touch me
Pay no attention to my stutter
Do not offer me an inhaler
It will not help
Asthma and panic attacks
Both affect breathing
But they require different treatment
My blood pressure is spiking
And an inhaler won't fix that
Telling me to calm down
Will not help
Asking me to get over it
Will be similarly ineffective
Forcing me to stop rocking
Will only make it worse
Trust me to know my body

I'm more familiar with it
Than you are

Dear everyone;
I owe you nothing
I do not owe you hugs
Or politeness
I do not owe you honesty
Or any of my time
I do not owe you an explanation
Or femininity
I do not have to tell you anything
My refusal is enough
It does not need qualifiers
If I do not want to do something
I do not have to
Regardless of how it makes you feel

I wrap my anger around me
Like a blanket
I use it to protect myself
Anger is a secondary emotion

It often covers fear
If I seem angry
It means that I am scared
Anger is easier to deal with
Than fear that leaves me paralyzed
The worst part is
Fear is a constant companion
It never leaves me for long
Always returns
To wreak havoc
I've spent so long in fear
That sometimes
I forget what it was like
To live life unafraid
I wonder what it must be like
To wake up everyday
Without fear
To go outside
Without thinking of risks
Or what could happen to you
What is it like to be
So cavalier

And go about your day
Feeling happy and safe
All the time?
I know it isn't normal
To feel this way
But it's normal for me
It's been this way for years
Still, I do my best
To try to fight my fears
I still leave the house sometimes
Still go places
And occasionally do things
Fear makes it harder to do things
But it isn't always impossible
It shouldn't take courage
To live

I wish things were different
Wish I could explain
How much of my life
Is dictated by my disorder
How PTSD has taken over me

Taught me to live a half-life
Always looking over my shoulder
Searching for the Sword of Damocles
Waiting to destroy me
Always prepared to have
The rug ripped out from
Underneath me
Never surprised when the Universe
Betrays me once again
I wish nobody understood
That no-one else
Ever felt this way
Alas, my wish is all for naught
Sadly; I am not alone
In this strange and sad existence
Far too many understand
Luckily some of them
Have left flashlights
And messages of hope
From when they too
Were trapped inside the dark
Wondering if sunlight

Was an illusion all along
If happiness was just a dream
Someone made up
To help them through the pain

Some of my dearest loved ones
Have gifted me with spoons
Shared their time with me
And sat beside me in the dark
In hopes that we would
Each see the dawn

I have never forgotten
The people who helped me
See another dawn
Nor will I
In the future
I wish them
My version of success
Which is to say
I wish them
Safety and happiness

Because if you are safe
But not happy
Than being safe
Cannot be enjoyed
And one cannot truly be happy
If one is not also safe
The two things belong together
And not enough people
Value either one

Frozen in my own skin
Trying to remember
To breathe
In and out
Surrounded by people
But feeling alone
Isolated by panic
Which has stolen
My voice
Life with my disorder
Is not a matter of choice
Life on repeat

Can feel like defeat
PTSD is like Dodgeball
A constant game
Of Fight, Flight, or Freeze
The only problem is
You can't tag out
Sometimes you see
What's coming in time to dodge
And other times
Something comes out of nowhere
Knocking you for a loop
Sometimes you feel
Like you're winning
Most days you're
Just trying to survive
The only way to win
Is to keep playing
Try to remember
That losing is not
The same as lost
You cannot know the score
Until the game is over

The hardest part
Is not the knockouts
It's getting up again
Ready for whatever
Win or lose
And still prepared to play

I want wolves and willow trees
Surrounding me
Howling at the moon
In the rain
Let the sky cry over me
Washing away my pain
As I tell the night
The truths too painful for day
Whisper fear into existence
In hopes that it too
Can be washed away

When the dawn breaks
My vigil will be over
And I will go to sleep

Certain that I will wake
And when I do
The cycle will begin anew

The trees are crying now
I might as well cry too
I wouldn't want them
To think their empathy was wasted
When it's the sweetest gift I've tasted
Will you cry with them too?
Or leave them to their silent vigil
If you water a plant
With your tears
When it's leaves fall
Is it crying for you?
I'm growing older
Without moving on
There's no next stage for me
I cannot change
I don't know how
To be anything but me
Or at least

This version of me

I barely remember

The me I used to be

They tell me I was happy once

And unafraid

Even if I believe them

About the happiness

I don't believe their claims

That I once felt no fear

I don't believe

That version of me

Ever truly existed

She sounds made up

Like a fairytale

Rather than me

If my childhood was a fairytale

It was definitely a Grimm one

My words are leaping off the page

And I'm left in a daze

As I wait for storms to pass

That are sparking in my brain

There is lightning in my mind
It reveals darker things inside
The truths I've tried to hide
Of all that I've been through
There's so much I still don't know
Of what occurred when I was young
I only know the horrors
Come when I am dreaming
And when I first awake
But when the daylight
Breaks my trance
The nightmares start to fade away
Hidden from the light of day

Someday I fear the truth will come
And refuse to hide itself once more
I fear that when it does
I will be no more
I think the truth will break me
And I will die once more
I don't know if I'll recover
Or who I'll become if I do

My past shapes my present
And I have died before
Only to awaken
Permanently altered
Unable to return
To who I was before
My mind frightens me
And I wish that wasn't true
But wishing cannot change the truth
And lies cannot remain forever
As time passes I remember more
Of what happened to me
When I was young and helpless
And each memory
Stokes the fires of rage
The heart of all my rage is fear
Nestled deep within

Is it wrong
That I should fear myself?
I've known for years
That there are things

I've suffered through
That I'm not brave enough to know
Horrors I've survived
That haunt my nightmares still
I'm haunting myself
My past is what wakes me screaming
The child I was
Is the reason I cry
And the woman I will never be
Is the reason for my fear
I wish I could say
That the reason those dreams died
Is because I outgrew them
Rather than the truth
It isn't that I changed my mind
It's that I broke
And when I did
The damage
Could not be undone
She is who I wanted to become
Instead I wound up
Locked inside my skin

Trapped in a never-ending battle
Trying to fight my brain
So that I can survive

I wish I could apologize
To younger versions of myself
For all that I failed to accomplish
And everything I can no longer do
There is little I could tell them
That would make it easier
To bear the truth of who I am
Still I would tell them
That we accomplished
Some of our dreams
That I never stopped writing
Or telling stories
And we can be proud of that
I'd tell them about love
And what it's like to feel safe
In someone else's arms
That not everyone will hurt us
And some even protect us from harm

I'd tell them words
Can be a weapon or a shield
And they will learn to use them as both
That even when the days are darkest
We will always be enough
Mostly I would hold them
And tell them I love them
And I'm sorry they have suffered alone
That if I could have stayed with them
To face it all
I would have
That they have always
Deserved to be protected
When my time with them was over
I'd return and tell myself the same thing
Although I suppose I already have
After all I'm writing this for me
And I will read it too

There's a lot that I don't share
And when I keep things to myself
It's not because I fear

Anyone's reaction
It's because I'm not comfortable
Sharing that information
At least not yet
There are things I've shared
That I never thought I would
And there are things I'll never say
Because the knowledge
Frightens me
These words are for your benefit
But I wrote them for me
I'm my target audience
And that means some things
Are only meant for me
I wonder why I share so much
Why this seems easier than talking
What is it about writing
That makes the truth spring forth
From the pen or from the page?
The text itself is black
And the page it's on is white
Even though the truth

Is often found in shades
At times I think my words
Should show up in vivid crimson
Because my poetry
Feels like bleeding
Ripping the truth from my brain
And spilling it all on the page

There is no relief
I must face this alone
Even when I'm not alone
I face my thoughts alone
I must face the past alone
No-one can fight these battles for me
And I would not wish them to
There's a certain honesty
In battling alone
I win or lose
On my own merits
In that I'm not alone
There's so much more to this
Than I have ever shown

I want you to know
Alone doesn't have to mean lonely
I can be a loner
And also be at peace
I don't mind the silence
As much as the noise
Inside my own head
It's not the isolation
It's being trapped in my own mind
That gets to me sometimes
I want to stay occupied
Because I'm afraid that if I don't
I'll be trapped inside my mind
It's my brain that I must battle
And my mind that I must save
Sometimes it feels hopeless
Since it's a war I'll never win
Even on the good days
I know bad days will return
Each battle won
Is a reminder
That the war

Will never end
Until I do

Sometimes it seems like
Trauma is my mother
And my father
That fear is my birthplace
And my ethnicity is hurt
My earliest memories
Are fear and shame
And so much pain
That it can never be fully expressed
I'm in a dark place now
I've been there before
And when I leave
I will return again
I always do
Because trauma is cyclical
It ebbs and flows
An ocean of pain
Following tides
No-one can control

Or predict

I want to set down roots

In the way only a transplant can

The way someone

Who moved too often

Longs to stay in one place

I am not a traveler

I do not get stir crazy

I wish I could paint the walls

Add a mural inside my home

Because I can

And there is no-one

To tell me not to

I have never painted my walls

Because they have

Never belonged to me

I think that's why

I add stickers

To my things

So I know that they are mine

Because even if someone else

Has the same thing

They won't decorate it
The way I do
What is it about decoration
That makes it feel
Like self expression?

I want myself to know
How much I've overcome
And how much I've left to do
This won't be an easy fight
But it's worth going through
There are dark days in my future
But there is also light
And I should not forget
That both of these are true
I'm holding fast
To memories
But holding faster
To the truth
Of who and what I am
I will fight

And I will carry on
Even when it seems impossible
I must remember
I have been through this before
And come out the other side
I won't say that it's easy
But it is possible
And that's enough for me
There's more strength in me
Than even I know
And if I remember that
My trials will be easier
Because I'll know
That I don't have to lose the fight
I just have to power through
And decide not to give up

It's time to close the door
On who I used to be
But the door
Will not stay shut

For long
No matter what I do
The past
Always comes through
Any barriers I make
Inside my mind
Since I can't pretend for long
I might as well be honest
And save myself some spoons

I'm living on spoon theory
And hiding from spoon thieves
But there are also spoon savers
That I call friends
It's a spoonie life for me
Yes a spoonie life for me
This part is silly
But it cost no spoons
So I'm gonna keep it
And call it a win
It's funny how vernacular
Can change the conversation

If I tell you that spoons
Mean energy
And being a spoonie
Means I'm chronically ill
Then it's a spoonie life for me
Takes on a different meaning
Because it's me saying:
It's a chronically ill life for me
Sometimes I think it would be easier
If it was my body that was broken
Instead of just my brain
Because than I'd only
Have to deal with my disability
Instead of also dealing with
Everyone's reaction to my disability
Being mentally ill
Is just as hard
As being physically ill
But fewer people understand
Or respect it
Which means I'm
Fighting a war on two fronts

I'm fighting my illness
And reactions to my illness
Good intentioned or not

If you think I've referenced
Mental health a lot in here
It's because I have
And it's intentional
Being mentally ill
And disabled as a result
Of said mental illness
Means that PTSD
Affects every aspect of my life
To varying degrees
This is no simple conundrum
That I can easily get past
It is the most important
Part of me
The part that everyone
I spend time with
Eventually comes to know

Each word I write

Paints a picture

Of my past

And my brain

Helps me uncover

Who I am

And who I've been

Shows me the truths

I've hidden from myself

And each piece of the puzzle

Paints a darker picture

Tells me more about the past

I can never fully escape

It's a Pandora's Box of horrors

That I know too much about

I can already piece

Some of it together

And the shadows

Are enough to haunt my dreams

Each word

Feels like a plea

A desperate attempt

To bargain with myself
As I try to unsee everything

I wish I was a blank slate
The past wiped clean
But that can never be
I will never be that free
I am trying to honor
The girl I used to be
To live my life
In a way
She would be proud of
One of us should
Get a chance to live
So I'll try
To be happy
For both of us

Some days it feels like a miracle
That I've survived
All of my yesterdays
And made it to today

Something few thought possible
It feels weird to live
Knowing others thought I wouldn't
It feels weirder
To be a success story
Because how could anyone
Look at me broken
And call that a success?
But living is winning
And I'm still alive
So I'm a success
I am still here
Despite all the pain
Despite my past
I am still here
I am still alive
And no-one
Can take that from me
Every day I wake up
Is a day that I win
Especially when
Waking up feels like failure

Every day I want to quit
And don't
Is a success
Anyone
Who tells you otherwise
Is lying

I am the Queen of Overthinking
The Master of Mistakes
If I'm gonna fall
It might as well
Be on my face
And if I have to fail
I'll do so with style

Sometimes breaking is all you can do
Sometimes the only thing breaking is you
Still there is love in the darkness
You're not walking alone
Somewhere in the dark
Someone's breaking with you
Somewhere in the darkness

Someone's heart is breaking in two
Somewhere in the dark
Someone's crying with you
Somewhere in the dark
Someone's searching for you
Somewhere in the dark
You're searching too

You are everything I've dreamed of
And never hoped to find
You know every part of me
There's nothing left to hide
You are my anchor in stormy seas
When things are darkest you comfort me

I'm tired of dreaming
When I'm still awake
I wake up still screaming
From memories I can't shake

After every rainstorm
There's a rainbow
Even the darkest night
Is broken by the dawn
So stay alive
And find your light
Whatever gets you
Through the night

A thousand tears
A thousand cries
Each one contains
A hurtful lie
You speak of safety
I know it not
Pain and rage
Have been my lot
The words flow onto the page
Like poison on a blade
I'll cut you yet
With sharpened truths
I was poisoned from the cradle

I drank hate like mothers' milk
No-one saved me as a child
No-one listened to my pleas
They just added to my files
I wasn't rescued
Until after I'd died
I'll never know
Who I could've been
If no-one hurt me as a child

We are roses
Damaged and broken
We try to reach the sky
Scared and scarred
We gift you with thorns
Our faith is shaken
Our trust was shattered
No longer are we innocent
It shows in our scars
Treat us with kindness
And we'll show you splendor
Unlike anything you've known

Incandescent pain
Beckons the rain
To spring from my eyes
And uncover the lies

The darkness is closing in
And I know that I can't swim
The light that burned so bright
Begins to dim
I don't know if I can win
But I still choose to fight

Poetry is about
Bleeding on the page
Slicing open your soul
And letting ink spill out
Revealing yourself
Letting readers and listeners alike
Get to know
The depths of your soul

An open mic night
Involves turning strangers
Into friends
As you discover
Things about them
You'd never learn
Any other way

When I stop writing
Time stretches out infinitely
Things hurt more
Pain takes over my being
I find it harder to wake up
As if writing is
One of the things I need
As necessary as
Food and sleep
One of my reasons
To stay alive

Never apologize
For who you were

It mattered then
So it matters now

I am lost
Like my siblings before me
We have different parents
But tell the same stories,
The same truths
When the truth is
People prefer the lies

They didn't love me
The first time they held me
They made no promises
Because mother's just a word
Like any other
It's a powerful ideal
But not a guarantee
And like a bird
I was shoved out of the nest
They didn't care if I could fly

I am more than your perceptions
Not a fan of self-deception
I just wanna find the key
To all my mysteries
The truth lies in the mirror
My reflection shows I'm haunted
By the ghosts of who I was
And who I can never be
The paths I can no longer travel
The people I won't grow to be
All of this
Is part of me
All of this
And so much more
My past and future
Haunt my present
And isn't that a present
That I never wanted

Even in my worst condition
I am more than my condition
I hope these words

Bring someone solace
That they find
Some comfort here

Sometimes I write
Poems to myself
Each line
A desperate cry for help
I pray I'll have the strength
To ask for
I write them crying
My face a mess
Trying to remind myself
That I've survived before
And I can do so again
That I won't always
Feel like this
That good days do exist
There are still
Things I've never done
I refuse to write a bucket list
I'm afraid if I do

I could finish it
And wind up
With one more reason
To die
I don't want to die
I just wish living
Didn't hurt so much
I'm holding on
By a thread
But I haven't let go
Living is the hardest thing
I will ever do
I want to live long enough
For all my hair
To turn grey

I live in the stillness
Between panic attacks
My cheeks more
Attuned to tears
Than blush
Sometimes I think

I was born scared
That I trembled
In the womb
Already accustomed
To the sounds
Of violence
Already aware
That I was not safe

Times are changing
Rearranging
And the only thing I know
Is that I don't wanna go
With the flow
If it means
Leaving myself behind
Or turning off
My conscience
Sometimes it hurts
To stand
Against the current
But that doesn't mean

It isn't worth it
Or that it can't be done
Cause there is value
In the work
Even when nobody sees it
And there are jobs
That can't be seen
Although their absence can

There are places
Where I cannot go
And things I cannot do
Although the reasons for that vary
And aren't always believed
There are truths
I've never told
Because I do not know them
Things about myself
That I have yet to learn
I try not lie
If it can be avoided
And lying to oneself

Seems a bigger crime
Than lying to another

There's a part of my heart
That can never be free
Because it doesn't belong to me
It belongs to the girl
That I used to be
And I owe her
Everything

Have you ever
Written words
So honest they hurt
Because they pulled
Truths from you
You never knew
You knew?

If you could
Bottle up potential

Would you save it

For a rainy day

Or give it all away?

From the time

We are born

Our options diminish

Each day

Bringing us closer

To a path

That seems set in stone

But isn't

The truth is

We can still

Chart a new course

But doing so

Becomes harder

As we grow

Set in our ways

It's harder to change

Once we've accepted our fates

Turned our lives

Into self-fulfilling prophecies

As we do
What we feel we must
What we are expected to
Blaming ourselves
When we do not fit the mold
Rather than embracing
Our unique selves

I'm trying to reconcile
The calming with the
Sea of Uncertainty
Swirling within me
There's so much
I still don't know
About myself
I've laughed,
And cried,
And almost died,
But even that
Is not the end
To all my mysteries

I want to be

More than my reflection

Thinks I can be

I was afraid

Of everything

I am trying

To succeed in my own way

I will fight

With every breath I take

To take another breath

And then another

Especially when it

Seems impossible

I love contradictions

And ordinary magic

I hate the way

Some people make me smaller

Shove me into boxes

The wrong size and shape for me

I've forgotten

The earliest hurts

And how to wear a dress

Without feeling uncomfortable
I remember the pain
And how it felt
To wear a hoodie
In August
I need to feel safe
And be my own best friend
I'm learning
To trust my body
After years of illness
Physical and mental
My brain's still sick
But my body's doing better

I define myself
More by what I'm not
Than what I am
And doesn't that make sense
Given my defiance
It's funny isn't it
How contrary
I choose to be

I don't hate labels
I never really did
I just hate being told
What label fits me best
If I'm going to be described
I should be able to choose
What terms apply
As I see fit
I also get to choose
When not to explain
Because my identity
Isn't up for debate
And whether I tell anyone
Which labels apply to me
Should always be my choice

Sleep is a forgotten memory
Or all I long to do
There's a world of truth
Between the two
It's time to close my eyes
And bid the waking world goodbye

So I can get some sleep tonight
Even if it isn't restful
I hope I don't remember anything
But even if I do
I'll still find a way
To make it through
I'm far too stubborn not to

I want to curl up in closets
And hide in confined spaces
Where no-one else can fit
I'm not claustrophobic
But I am agoraphobic
The smaller the space
The safer I feel
I spend a lot of time hiding
From my mind
Trying to distract myself
From the things
I think and feel
In hopes that it won't
Hurt as much

I'm gonna
Write my own story
Add a chapter
In the book
I call my life
And in the process
I'll flesh out my character
And learn things about myself
I've figured out my motivations
And who I want to be
There's no villain I can see
No new monsters left to face
Save the ones inside my brain
That haunt me to this day
Sometimes I feel like
A sidekick to myself
As if my story isn't mine
Only support for someone else
Who's meant for something more
Than I can even dream of
Not that I know who

I'd be the sidekick to
Since it's nearly impossible
To see the impact
That we have on others
Like ripples in a pond
Our influence on others
Grows greater over time
So even if my life
Exists just to
Bolster someone else
That doesn't mean
It has no value
Or that I have no worth

Sometimes I want to
Write a love letter to me
Tell myself that I
Deserved better
Than the childhood I got
That I shouldn't have learned
The lessons I got

In cruelty
That the tears I've shed
Over my past
Are not a sign of weakness
And my anger
Over how I was treated
Is because I know
That it should not have happened
I feel indignant
When I think about my past
But full of rage
When I think
Of it happening to someone else
And that is sadder
Than the fact it happened
I shouldn't be
More outraged for another
Than I ever was for me
I deserve to be mad
On my own behalf

It's time to write
Let your muse take flight
Pick up a pen
And spill out your soul
I will teach you
Emotions we don't
Have names for
That can only be learned
By studying the contradictions
Involved in the human condition
Things I learned from writing
About how I see the world
And what that's taught me
About others

Sometimes it seems
I'm running out of time
To figure out my life
As if there's an expiration date
That only I can sense
But I know that's a lie
It's only in my mind

So I decide to write
I'm working out my feelings
With every word I type
I'm closer to an answer
As I try to solve
My mysteries
Because even if I fail
To unlock them all
The trying teaches me
Things I never would have known
About myself
Any other way

There's a chance
I'll figure myself out
Someday
But it will not be today
Because I'm
Unraveling the tapestry
That makes up my life
I can't see where it started
But I've found

Some common threads

And a few repeated patterns

And I know

If I could see it all

It would be beautiful

And horrifying

To varying degrees

I don't know which

Would strike me first

Or which one would be greater

But that doesn't really matter

I'm still trying to

Untangle my motivations

And figure out

Who I want to be

Not that I'll ever

Know the latter

Because it changes

All the time

Who am I?

Is a universal,

Timeless question

Because it changes rapidly
Everyone becomes themselves
Over time
And who that is,
Is never static
It changes with the tides
I am more myself
Today than I was yesterday
And tomorrow
I'll be more so
Than today

I'm staring at four walls
Wondering why they never close in
You'd think I'd learn to hate them
But I find it comforting
I know this place is mine
Even if it's not forever
At least it's mine for now
And even when I know
I can't leave
It's easy for me

Because I don't want to
Outside has people
Who can't be predicted
I never know
What they will do
Or how it will affect me
And that terrifies me
I'm trying to fight my fears
And stave off paranoia
But it isn't easy
When there's so many reasons
That I should be afraid
I don't want to explain them all
I'm not sure I should have to
After all, it's not my fault
That I was taught to fear
I'm not brave
And I wouldn't say I'm reckless
I value self-preservation
In ways that only
The traumatized can
My past has left its mark on me

You could say it's
Stained my soul
I am the picture
Of fear on a bad day
On a good one
I might be the picture
Of resilience

This ends how it starts
With poetry
And a time limit
The words come faster under pressure
And deadlines
Create new stanzas
So I'm writing
To unburden my soul
And letting out my feelings
All of this is true
Even if some of it is fiction

I'm using metaphors
And similes
To express
All the things
I long to say
But lack the words for
Sometimes approaching things
From a different angle
Makes it easier to
Find the right solution
Now that it's almost over
I almost think I'll miss it
But all this self-reflection
Has to end some time
And it might as well be now
I've learned a lot
About myself
From writing this
And promising
Not to edit it
To make myself look better
The truth isn't always pretty

But the lies hurt more
There's so much more to say
But that's another story
For another day

I'm trying to unbind myself
From expectations
Including the ones
I placed upon myself
I don't have to be
Anything I'm not
And that's okay
As long as I can
Look myself in the mirror
And not hate who I've become

Made in the USA
Middletown, DE
11 April 2023